WHATEVER: CHRISTIAN DATING IN A SECULAR WORLD

Copyright © 2012 Ryan C. Vet

Unless otherwise indicated, all Scripture quotations are from *The Holy Bible, New International Version*®. *NIV*®. Copyright ©1973, 1978, 1984, 2011 by International Bible Society.

Cover Design and Interior Layout by Ryan C. Vet

ISBN 978-1470010201

Printed in the United States of America

Second Edition, 2012

Jessica,
Thank you for showing me how rewarding dating can be
when living in the freedoms of God's boundaries.

Glad we are on the same page.

"Finally, brothers and sisters, whatever is true, whatever is noble, whatever is right, whatever is pure, whatever is lovely, whatever is admirable—if anything is excellent or praiseworthy—think about such things."

Philippians 4:8

Contents

Introduction

God has given us the incredible gift of freedom as Christ followers. We can live free knowing that we can cast all of our cares on Christ and that the punishment for our sins was taken upon our Lord and Savior, Jesus Christ, as he hung on the cross with his arms stretched out, being mocked and ridiculed by spectators as he suffocated and with his last breath uttered, "It is finished," culminating his ministry here on earth.

This incredible gift of God's grace through his son has given us, as believers, unparalleled freedom. The Bible is not a list of do's and don't's for Christians. Instead, the Bible is God's infallible Word that serves as a guideline and puts boundaries in place to help Christ-followers as they pursue a righteous, Christ-centered life.

As Christians, we often look to the Bible as a magic crystal ball that is supposed to provide us with clear, black and white answers to our future, reveal God's will and give us clear direction in the choices we are to make. Though God gives us direction through his Word, he also gives us so much freedom in making our own decisions ranging from choosing a college to choosing who we will date and ultimately who we will marry.

In the very beginning of the Bible, God created the first man and the first woman--Adam and Eve. In Genesis 2, the Garden of Eden is described as a lush garden filled with beauty and splendor, created by God for man to enjoy. God's rules for living and indulging in the magnificence of the Garden were so simple, "You are free to eat from any tree in the garden; but you must not eat from the tree of the knowledge of good and evil, for when you eat from it you will certainly die." Genesis 2:16-17. From the very beginning, God gave man incredible freedoms to explore the beauty and creation that he gave to humankind. That independence was simply governed by the simple rule, "Don't eat from the tree of the knowledge of good and evil." Often when God gives us a command that is to be followed he offers an explanation of why. His explanation to Adam and Eve was simple, "For when you eat from it you will surely die."

In the same way, God has given similar parameters to Christ-followers today that allow us to explore and enjoy his creation and to bring us pleasure.

He has given us simple rules to which we must adhere in order to fully appreciate the wondrous works of his mighty hand that he so generously passed on to us to delight in. This includes dating relationships. We, as believers are allowed to exercise our liberties by using all that God has given us, and on occasion, he puts parameters around certain actions, behaviors and thoughts to protect us from getting hurt.

This book is designed to be a tool for young, Christian couples that desire to have a Christ-centered, healthy and pure dating relationship. Establishing a foundation in your relationship with God's Word as the cornerstone allows Christian couples to bask in the freedom of knowing that they will be able to live in pure joy, delighting in the beauty and pleasures brought about by the opposite sex to whom they are attracted. The satisfaction and rewards of a dating relationship can be achieved all while feeling comforted by the peace of knowing that their relationship is pure and free of regrets because it is in accordance with the truths found in the Bible.

This study, entitled *Whatever*, stems from one of my favorite passages in Scripture found in Paul's letter to the church at Philippi in Philippians 4:8 saying "Finally, brothers and sisters, whatever is *true*, whatever is **noble**, whatever is **right**, whatever is **pure**, whatever is **lovely**, whatever is **admirable**—if anything is **excellent or praiseworthy**—think about such things." Though this study is not exclusively a study in the book of Philippians, it is based off of the values found in Philippians 4:8. I feel this title is so fitting because in our culture, it seems that people often have the mindset that "whatever happens, happens" when talking about relationships. "If having sex outside of marriage is what culture says, then whatever, let's do it." It is easy to be flippant about relationships or get so engulfed by the passion in a single moment that we lose sight of our end-goal as Christians in dating--finding the one individual who you will ultimately spend the rest of your life with. This study's goal is to help Christian couples find common ground in Christ by examining whatever is true, noble, right, pure, lovely, admirable, excellent and praiseworthy in their relationship with one another.

GOD'S STANDARD FOR DATING

Just as God gave Adam and Eve one simple command in the Garden of Eden, so he gives us as Christ-followers one simple criterion and prerequisite for the person we are to date found in 2 Corinthians 6:14, "Do not be yoked together with unbelievers. For what do righteousness and wickedness have in common? Or what fellowship can light have with darkness?"

This passage is not dealing solely with dating and marriage relationships, it also is referring to the bigger picture of relationships including relationships such as business partnerships. It is important in reading Scripture to fully understand the context surrounding the passage that is being read as well as trying to understand the background and history of the passage.

This passage is written by the Apostle Paul and to the church in Corinth known for their wild and rambunctious tendencies. In writing these words, Paul is creating a metaphorical parallel between the Old Testament Law of Moses and everyday human relationships inferring that relationships, specifically romantic relationships, should be between two individuals that are at the same point in their Christian journey. In Deuteronomy 22:10, the Old Testament Laws states that a donkey can not be yoked to a plow with an ox nor a clean animal with an unclean animal. The reason is simple, an ox, typically weighing 2000 pounds, is substantially larger and stronger than the average donkey weighing a mere 500 pounds. If you strap them together in front of a plow, the ox will most certainly pull the donkey along, slowing the ox down and causing friction and conflict between the two animals.

As Paul uses this illustration, he is trying to very clearly illustrate the importance of being in a relationship with an individual that is at the same place you are spiritually so that as you move forward together, you can challenge each other and encourage one another to fall more in love with God everyday.

Though the Bible only has one clear perquisite on Christian's dating other believers, there is an endless list of standards and principles from purity to honesty to true love, that God's Word is very clear on. Hopefully this study will give you and your partner a chance to really dive into God's Word and try to understand God's standards in Christian dating relationships.

God has given us incredible freedom in choosing the individual that we will ultimately marry with the one stipulation of marrying a Christian. This freewill is simultaneously exciting and terrifying. The tale of our lives is like one of those custom story books that has your name written in it and there are different points throughout the story where you can choose one path or the other. Those paths are representative of different people you could date and decisions you make with that individual. Ultimately there are several different endings to your story, none are necessarily wrong or outside of God's plan for you. God is the author of the story, so no ending you choose goes against his perfect plan so long as the choice you make is governed by the truths of God's Word. Throughout this study, you will have the opportunity to engage in some deep conversations with your boyfriend or girlfriend that will help the two of you to really determine some of the paths you will take throughout your dating relationship.

USING THIS STUDY

Building a foundation that is firmly is rooted in God's Word is the single most critical element in a Christian dating relationship. Imagine building a house without the support of the load-bearing beam running through the structure. Though the building may stand for a while, it will ultimately cave in under the pressures of being lived in day after day. In the same way, relationships without Christ and God's Word at the very center are destined to crumble and be full of discontent and unhappiness.

Keeping your individuality as well as managing your relationship with your significant other is a delicate balance and can often be difficult to juggle.

Through this study, make sure that you focus on God's Word as an individual. Spend time completely alone, away from the distractions of your phone and the Internet and focus fully on what God wants you to learn from his Word. This time alone with God is crucial in your spiritual walk. It can be difficult to advance spiritually and strengthen your relationship with our Lord and Savior if you rely too much on your boyfriend or girlfriend to grow with you. Instead, you must make sure that your vertical relationship with God is strong and is growing deeper daily before you can have effective horizontal relationships here on this earth. Even though growing together spiritually as a couple is important, you will ultimately struggle down the road if you use your companion as a crutch and as the only source of growth and getting fed spiritually.

This book is composed of eight different studies, each with an overarching theme derived from the book of Philippians, specifically the verse Philippians 4:8. In each individual study, you will find six subheadings: *In The Word, Alone with God, Together before God, Prayer Points, Application* and *Memorization*. Each section is designed to be used to help you to grow individually in your walk with Christ as well as allow room for you and your partner to challenge one another to grow spiritually. Each subheading is described in further detail below:

IN THE WORD: Every lesson has several passages of Scripture that you should read individually and reflect on. Though the passages can be read all at once, it is ideal to spread them out, or reread them throughout the course of a week.

ALONE WITH GOD: These are a series of questions that you should answer individually, apart from your boyfriend or girlfriend. This is a chance for you to think very carefully on what you believe is true about God's Word and how it is applicable in your own life. These questions should be answered throughout the course of the week instead of all at once. The questions do not need to be answered in order. When you review the study as a couple, you may want to share some of your answers to these questions with one another, though sometimes these answers may be best for your own reflection.

TOGETHER BEFORE GOD: These are a series of simple questions that you are to ask your companion when you are together and are reviewing the lesson.

This will allow you to both express your views on the Scripture you have studied over the past week and it will allow you to find common ground in God's Words as well as discuss any differences of opinion or interpretation you may have.

PRAYER POINTS: Prayer is pivotal to having open communication with God. Prayer Points encourages you to pray specifically for things within your own life as well as pray for your relationship. It is good to pray in private as well as pray openly with one another. It is encouraged that both individuals pray out loud together when they meet to review and learn from the study.

APPLICATION: These are simple practical ways in which you can put what you have learned into action in your own life. There is also room for you to add your own ideas of how to apply what you have learned during that study.

MEMORIZATION: As Christ-followers, it is so important that we hide God's Word in our hearts. Each study contains relevant scripture that the couples should try to memorize together each week.

A Look at Philippians

n order to understand Philippians 4:8, the verse that this entire study primarily focuses on, it is important to grasp the background and context of the entire book of Philippians. This first study will take you on a walk through Philippians and give you an overview of the history of the book.

While being under house arrest awaiting trial before the ruler of Rome at the time, Emperor Nero, the Apostle Paul, received a visitor named Epaphroditus. Epaphroditus came from the church in Philippi to bring a report on the latest happenings in the church as well as a gift for furthering Paul's ministry. Epaphroditus returned to the Church of Philippi with the Letter of Philippians from the Apostle Paul and co-authored by Timothy.

Despite being imprisoned, Paul urges the church at Philippi to rejoice always. Throughout the letter, Paul imparts wisdom of what it truly means to live a godly life and what it means to imitate Christ.

In the letter, Paul and Timothy outline a plethora of ideas and principles that Christ-followers should apply to their daily life with everyone that they rub shoulders with. These concepts are also very important for us to examine as we embark on a Christian relationship journey. The book of Philippians is filled with practical insights covering the spectrum of living a Christ-centered life. These nuggets of wisdom are all fundamental stepping-stones in a God-fearing dating relationship.

IN THE WORD

Philippians 1

Philippians 2

Philippians 3

Philippians 4

As you read through the book of Philippians, take time to meditate on key verses and concepts. It would be a great idea to keep a separate journal where you can record your thoughts and really dive into God's Word throughout the course of this study.

ALONE WITH GOD

How would you expand on the idea of living a life that is worthy of the Gospel?

What do you think it means to work out your salvation with fear and trembling?

Do you feel that being selfless and humble play a role in a Christian dating relationship? Why? How?

Does being in a relationship focus your mind too much on earthly things to the point that you are distracted from being fully focused on God?

Do you currently manage your thought life to think on whatever is true, right, noble, pure, lovely, admirable, excellent and praiseworthy in line with what it says in Philippians 4:8?

After reading the entire book of Philippians, what are some of the main themes in the book?

What things bring you joy in life?

Do you feel that the way I treat you exemplifies Christ's humility and that I put your interests and desires above my own?

Does being in a relationship with me distract you from growing closer and more intimate with God or does it spur you on to developing a relationship with our Savior and Creator?

Paul speaks of his own trials and warns against being anxious. How do you react in situations of high stress and how can I help point you to God and encourage you as a brother or sister-in-Christ during those times?

Does the way in which we govern our relationship accurately reflect the fact that we are followers of Christ?

PRAYER POINTS

God, I pray that today you will teach me to be humble, putting others above myself.

Lord, I pray that today my life will reflect you and that I will live in a manner the represents your Gospel both in what I say and what I do.

Father, thank you for sending your son Jesus Christ to take on the punishment for our sins. Help me to put aside my own desires for things of this world and lusts of this flesh for you.

I praise you for my boyfriend/girlfriend and the relationship you have blessed us with. Help our relationship to keep you center and first in all things that we do. May we never lose sight of your love for us.

APPLICATION

Go through this devotional book and write all of the Scripture that is to be memorized on note cards so that you can start reviewing them. This could be a fun activity to do as a couple.

This week, be consciously aware of others and make it a point to put others above yourself. Simply do something small everyday for a complete stranger or a close friend, that causes you to think about their well-being and desires above your own.

Set up an opportunity where you and your companion can serve together. It can be in your neighborhood or community, at your church or maybe even planning on participating on a group missions trip or service trip.

⚬ ⚬ ⚬ ⚬ ⚬ MEMORIZATION ⚬ ⚬ ⚬ ⚬ ⚬

Philippians 2:3-4

"Do nothing out of selfish ambition or vain conceit. Rather, in humility value others above yourselves, not looking to your own interests but each of you to the interests of the others."

Philippians 4:8

"Finally, brothers and sisters, whatever is true, whatever is noble, whatever is right, whatever is pure, whatever is lovely, whatever is admirable— if anything is excellent or praiseworthy—think about such things."

Whatever is True

In Philippians 4:8, the word "true" that Paul uses is the Greek word, *alethes*. This Greek word translated to today's English means real or authentic. Establishing a basis of being true and authentic in your Christian dating relationship is fundamental and foundational to growing closer as a couple and more importantly, growing independently closer to God.

Being true is the basic building block of trust. Trust and true-openness go hand-in-hand. Truthfulness and being true sound similar to one another but have completely different connotations. The idea of truthfulness is merely telling the truth. If a question is asked, the truthful person would give an honest answer. Whereas the idea of *being true* gets down to the core of a person's thoughts, attitudes and actions. Being true, the type of "trueness" referred to in this passage, is talking about being completely authentic and real— totally being yourself and being truly open. Being true is not a noun like truth, it is a verb that should be applied to your lifestyle.

Most people, myself included, often mask our true selves. In psychology, the way we portray ourselves is known as our self-awareness and self-presentation. These terms refer to the idea that we control who we are and how we act in various situations. When we are with our family, we will act a particular way and when we are with friends, teachers, co-workers or bosses we act in a completely different manner. When we alter the way we act for different people, we are hiding who we truly are. Inadvertently, this masking is caused by our insecurities and fears that people will not appreciate us for who we truly are--our passions, desires and ambitions. As a result, we put up a wall that only allows our friends or family to see a certain side of us as we monitor our actions so that we can have full control of what people see on the outside instead of being vulnerable and allowing people to see us for who we are on the inside.

Every single person on planet earth has quirks and nuances that make them unique. Each one of us has our own story and has different experiences that make us who we are today. Some of those differences, idiosyncrasies and experiences are funny and they are something that can be laughed at. On the other hand, some of the events in your past can haunt you day in and day out because maybe you were hurt or betrayed by someone you felt safe with, or maybe you had your trust shattered by someone you loved or maybe your sweet innocence was stolen by someone who promised you everything was going to be okay.

Those circumstances are what make us who we are. Your history from the happiest moments to the darkest days compounds and builds to make you into the person you are today. In order for you to exercise this principle of being true and authentic, you need to be willing to be open with your boyfriend or girlfriend. You need to be able to laugh together and cry together. You need to be able to listen and be able to talk. Being true is the ongoing act of open communication. If you pick up any literature on relationships, dating or otherwise, open communication is often the key component to a successful relationship.

To be truly open and vulnerable, you must fully trust your companion and they must be able to trust you. Getting to the point as a couple where you feel you can truly talk about your emotions and feelings is not something that happens magically when you first start dating. Trust takes time to build and ultimately being real and authentic with one another is a process and a journey.

God's Word talks so much about honesty and the truth as well as how important it is to talk openly with close friends including your significant other. Though being open as a couple is vital to a healthy relationship, it is also equally, if not more important to have someone of the same gender that can act as an accountability partner--a person that can totally relate to your struggles and your temptations and be able to talk openly and offer you sound, godly advice. Despite the fact that being open with your boyfriend or girlfriend is crucial, there are some things that are better discussed and hashed out with an accountability partner.

This idea of being true must be governed by the truths found in God's Word. As a couple, you must not only be true to one another, but you must be true to God and act in accordance with what he has outlined for you, as his child. If you use the Bible as a guide and a spiritual compass in your dating relationship, it will help diminish the likelihood for disagreements based on faith and belief. Staying authentic and open with one another and remaining true to God's Word will exponentially increase a couple's chances of dealing with hard issues and conflicts in a manner that is Christ-like. Pure open honesty is a surefire way to avoid conflicts that could arise in a relationship because one person wasn't telling the whole truth or because they were hiding a secret or a key part of a larger story. The truth may sting. However, the sting caused by being true from the beginning is far less severe than the pain inflicted from uncovering a secret months or even years into a relationship.

Throughout the Scriptures you will read in this study of the course of the next week, you will be focusing on both God's truths found in his Word as well as being true and open as a couple. This idea of being true is an ongoing choice of being authentic, even when it is hard and awkward. Being true from the beginning and dwelling on whatever is true in your dating relationship will help build a platform with your partner that will allow you to discuss absolutely anything in grace, love and mercy.

Do you feel that you are at a point where you can be totally open and honest with your partner? How can you continue to maintain a relationship driven by God's truth and being true to one another?

Is there an individual in your life outside of your boyfriend or girlfriend that you can totally confide in and look to for sound wisdom and godly advice? Who is it?

The tongue is powerful as James 3 talks about. How do you use your tongue to be an instrument for positive change, truthfulness and encouragement?

Are you careful about letting your "yes" be yes and your "no" be no? Why do you think that this is an important concept to put into practice in your life?

Think of a time when you rejoiced in your companion's excitement and felt empathy in their sorrow. In these moments of emotion, both good and bad, do you turn to the Lord and pray to him or praise him for what he has done?

● ● ● ● **TOGETHER BEFORE GOD** ● ● ● ●

Do you feel that I am totally open with you?

Do you feel that being in a relationship has helped you grow in your walk with Christ?

When you are sad, do you feel that I listen and empathize? When you are happy, do you feel that I truly share in your joy?

No matter how painful the truth may be, do you feel that you can honestly tell me anything without fearing I will show you unrighteous anger?

Is there anything that you have not told me that I should know that could affect our relationship?

PRAYER POINTS

God, thank you for giving us your Word as a beacon of truth that shines out on our lives. Help your perfect, holy Word to govern my life and govern my relationship.

Lord, help me to be true. I pray that you will allow me to be open in this relationship so that this relationship will not be hindered by secrets or suppressed feelings. Help me to be authentic and real.

Father, teach me how to be excited when my partner is excited and empathize when my companion feels hurt and pain. Help me to be a good listener and offer your truths as guidance through both the bright and the dark times.

● ● ● ● ● **APPLICATION** ● ● ● ● ● ●

This week make it a point to be open and true-to-self. Throw out your insecurities and tell your companion something that makes you feel insecure, nervous or fearful in life that he or she may not already know about you and be willing to talk about it.

Every day this week, come up with a fun fact that makes you unique and tell your boyfriend or girlfriend. This can get be a great way to learn little things about each other that may not ordinarily come up in daily conversation.

If you do not already have an accountability partner (someone of the same gender, age and spiritual maturity) start praying and heavily considering finding someone that you can share life with and someone that will challenge you and hold you accountable to God's standards for your life.

1 Thessalonians 5:11

"Therefore encourage one another and build each other up, just as in fact you are doing."

James 1:19-20

"My dear brothers and sisters, take note of this: Everyone should be quick to listen, slow to speak and slow to become angry, because human anger does not produce the righteousness that God desires."

Whatever is Noble

ossibly the hardest thing that Christian couples face in today's culture is not succumbing to the pressures that the world puts on dating. Often the world's idea of relationships does not align with God's boundaries for us as Christ-followers in regards to dating. While society's standards seem so attractive and pleasurable, the long-term repercussions of not abiding by God's Word will leave you as an individual and you both as a couple left longing for something that you cannot have outside of God's perfect parameters of marriage.

The idea of nobility in Philippians 4:8 refers to being reputable and honorable. Another word that could be used to describe this concept is integrity. Integrity is one of those buzzwords that parents have emphasized to their children, schools have utilized in honor codes and politicians can't seem to figure out its true meaning. The idea of integrity is easy to talk about but far more difficult to put into practice. Integrity simply means doing the right thing in accordance with the truths found in God's Word regardless of who is looking.

God blesses people of integrity. This is seen throughout the Bible time and time again. One of the best illustrations of integrity, specifically in regards to purity, is the story of Joseph and Potiphar's wife. Joseph was a young, attractive man. He immediately gained favor in the eyes of his master's wife. Time after time, Potiphar's wife tried to get Joseph to come and sleep with her. Despite her persistence, Joseph resisted. At one point, he literally fled her presence leaving his garment in her hands because he refused to sin against God and against Potiphar. The manipulative woman conjured up a story claiming that Joseph was forcing himself upon her. This caused Joseph to face serious consequences.

Joseph was noble and did the right thing despite the stories and lies being told about him. Deep down in his heart, Joseph knew that he was not at fault despite the fact he was taking the blame for a sin which he did not commit. Joseph was honorable and upheld his reputation so that no bad thing could be truthfully said about him. In the same way, we should live out our lives and our relationships in such a way that no bad thing can truthfully be said about us.

As you will read, God showed favor to Joseph because of his nobility and his desire to do what is right. Not only did Joseph show integrity through his actions in the instance with Potiphar's wife, but also later in his dealings with his brothers who betrayed him and left him for dead just years earlier. Joseph's story is a prime example of how we should practice integrity in every facet of our life.

Honor is another word that can be interchanged with "noble" in Philippians 4:8. One of the most familiar verses in the Bible containing the word honor is found in Ephesians 6:2 saying, "honor your father and mother." Honoring God in a Christian dating relationship seems pretty straightforward. However, considering the idea that you, as a child, are called to honor your parents in everything you do, including dating, adds a new perspective into the mix. You are placed in the care of your parents until you leave your father and mother and are joined with a spouse in marriage (Genesis 2:24). Your earthly father and mother have been put over you as authority figures by God and you are to respect them as you go about your relationship with your companion. As it says in Romans 13, you are to respect the authorities that God has given us.

So what exactly does honoring your father and mother look like while dating? The answer is not clear cut. As a young couple, it is often easy to get excited with your relationship you accidently (or maybe purposefully) leave your parents out of the loop. You may struggle with telling them things that are going on in your life as it is. Maybe the last thing you want is to let your parents know the details of your relationship status. However, as their child, despite your desire to be independent, if you are truly honoring your parents and if you want your relationship with your boyfriend or girlfriend to be honoring to God, it is important that you keep your parents clued in. Be open in communication and respect their wishes. In no way does this mean you need to give our parents a running log of your daily activities with your partner or a printout of all letters, messages and texts sent back forth as well as a transcript of phone conversations. Instead, you need to be sensitive to what your parents want to know and be willing to honor their authority in your life. This idea of honor and integrity with parents will look different for every couple.

Talking to guys for a minute, you are supposed to be spiritual leaders in your dating relationship and ultimately in your marriage. You need are accountable before God for the actions you take in your relationship. One of the greatest ways to demonstrate nobility is to honor your girlfriend's parents by taking the time to talk to them. Let them know just how much you respect their daughter and desire to maintain a godly relationship. Man up and sit down with your girlfriend's father and let him know that you desire to respect his daughter and care for her and put her best interest first. And, if you really want to exemplify honor and be a noble young man, you will ask the tough question, "Sir, do you have any requests in terms of the way I treat your daughter?" As long a you and your girlfriend are not married, you must submit to your girlfriend's parents authority. You are responsible for honoring your girlfriend, honoring her parents, honoring your parents and most importantly, honoring God.

Now back to guys and girls, being a person of integrity and being noble can be difficult. The concept of being reputable should be consist throughout every area of your dating relationship. Integrity impacts your horizontal relationships with friends, family, parents and with one another as well as the vertical relationship between you as an individual and as a couple with God, our Heavenly Father.

Live out your relationship in such a way that you do not care who is looking. You should never be ashamed of your actions. Practice being noble in both your thoughts and your actions towards your companion demonstrating respect, honor and care.

This week's study takes you through the adult life of Joseph. While reading and studying these chapters, try concentrating on Joseph's noble actions from making the wise choices with Potiphar's wife to the way he ultimately treated his brothers with grace and forgiveness despite the fact they had severely wronged him.

IN THE WORD
Genesis 39 - 45
1 Thessalonians 4:1-12

How would you define integrity?

Does the way you live your life change depending on who is watching? If so, why do you think that is?

When temptation arises, how do you plan to exemplify integrity?

Do you view God and his Word as your ultimate authority? What impact does that view have on the way you live your life?

At the end of the day, would your friends, family, co-workers, employers and teachers say that one of your character traits is integrity? If not, how could you further exercise being a person of integrity?

As Christ-followers, we are sons and daughters of the King. Do you feel that the way you live your life reflects your noble roots?

When you are faced with a situation that could compromise your honor, what escapes routes do you have in place that will help you maintain your integrity?

● ● ● ● **TOGETHER BEFORE GOD** ● ● ● ●

Do you think our relationship is grounded in integrity and is honorable?

As people look from the outside in, do you think we are perceived as a couple that exemplifies integrity?

In what ways did Joseph demonstrate integrity?

Do we live in such a way, using God's Word as our one and only standard, that others would view our relationship in a positive light thinking that we honor God in our actions towards one another?

Do you think that I honor your parents and God in the way I treat you?

Do you feel like I treat you with integrity, honor and respect?

● ● ● ● ● **PRAYER POINTS** ● ● ● ● ●

Lord, thank you for the true story of Joseph and his example of living out integrity even when it hurts. I pray that you will help me to be a person of integrity so that I will do the right thing in accordance with your Word regardless of who is watching.

When temptations are dangled in front of me, it can be tough to do the right thing. I pray that you will give me the strength to overcome temptations.

Heavenly father, I pray that you will help me learn to honor you as well as my significant other and my parents and their parents as I pursue a Christ-centered relationship.

APPLICATION

Guys, if you have not yet talked to your girlfriend's father or legal guardian, do it. Honor them in that way.

Send a letter home to your parents this week letting them know how much you appreciate them. It is a small, but powerful way to show honor.

MEMORIZATION

Ephesians 6:1-3

"Children, obey your parents in the Lord, for this is right. 'Honor your father and mother'—which is the first commandment with a promise— 'so that it may go well with you and that you may enjoy long life on the earth.'"

Whatever is Right

Righteousness as well as its antonym, unrighteousness, are two topics that are frequently addressed throughout both the Old and the New Testaments. Righteousness is one of those "Christian" terms that is often thrown around, but maybe not fully understood. So what does righteousness mean? Mariam Webster defines righteousness as "acting in accord with divine or moral law; free from guilt or sin." This definition is dead on and fully encompasses what it means to be righteous. Our behaviors, in mirroring the life of Christ Jesus, should be free from guilt and free from sin and we should adhere to the divine law (God's Word) as the direction for our lives and the lamp onto the path of our relationships.

Scattered throughout the Bible there are stories of men and women who have been found righteous in the eyes of God. These are men and women who have done exactly as God instructed them to do through his laws and commands. In Hebrews 11, known as "The Hall of Faith," Able, the son of Adam and Eve is referred to as "a righteous man" because his heart pure and true. Able desired with all of his heart to please the Lord in everything he did. In the same way, in order to be found righteous in our dating relationship, we must be obedient to what God has outlined for us in his Word.

It can become extremely easy to get wrapped up in becoming legalistic and segmenting the Bible into a list of do's and don't's. In reality, there are certain issues in the Bible that do not have a definitive right or definitive wrong answer. This is where the line of being righteous can be extremely difficult to interpret, especially within a dating relationship. When, as an individual or as a couple, you come up against an issue that appears to have no clear answer of what is righteous or not, you often find yourself asking, "What is the right thing to do in this situation?"

Well, if the Bible isn't clear on an issue, who are we, as humans, to decide what is ultimately right and wrong? We aren't able to make that call. There is only one Judge and that is God who ultimately declares something as righteous or unrighteous. When an issue falls into this preverbal "gray area" it can be easy to try and see how far you can go without sinning. In these instances, you need to step back and get away from asking, "What is the right thing to do?" and instead you need to change the question to ask, "What is the wise thing to do based on God's Word in light of my current situation?" When you come up to an issue where there is no apparent black and white answer, you need to exercise wisdom.

The book of Proverbs, or "The Book of Wisdom" as it is often referred to, is a book full of wise sayings for the righteous. There are going to be countless times throughout your life whether in your dating relationship or elsewhere that will leave you scratching your head wondering what is right and wrong. In order to be righteous, you need to be firmly rooted in your faith. There will be times, more often than not, when doing the right thing is the most unattractive option. Sometimes, as Christ-followers, doing the right thing will get us mocked and persecuted. But as Jesus said in his Sermon on the Mount found in Matthew 5, "Blessed are those who hunger and thirst for righteousness for they will be filled...blessed are those who are persecuted for righteousness, because theirs is the kingdom of heaven."

As a Christ-follower, you should hunger and thirst to do what is right and wise in accordance with God's standards. Going back to the very beginning, God gives us as his children so much freedom like he did for Adam and Eve. When God issues out a standard by which we are supposed to live, it is to protect us and not to harm us (Jeremiah 29:11).

We are all sinners. Every single human being that has ever walked this earth, with the exception of Jesus Christ, has sinned and has fallen short of the glory of God. We are not worthy enough to inherit the kingdom of heaven on our own. But, by God's grace through sending his perfect, righteous son, we have been given new life in Christ. As a result, our Redeemer and Rescuer bore our sins so that we "might become the righteousness of God," 2 Corinthians 5:21 and ultimately have the gift of eternal life with our Father in heaven.

It is because of that incredible gift of grace that you can celebrate your freedom in Christ. As a Christ-follower, righteousness is obtained through your faith in Jesus Christ as you will read this week in Romans 3. Your faith goes hand-in-hand with being righteous. Christians do not have a relationship with Jesus Christ because of the righteous things they have done or because they have observed the law. They have a relationship with their heavenly Father because of their faith and belief that he—out of his mercy and goodness—sent his one and only son to carry our sin to the cross. It is because of that faith we are able to live and think rightly.

As you read this week, you will see examples of men and women of faith in Hebrews 11 and how they acted in righteousness. You will also read one of the most famous passages in all of Scripture on the topic of righteousness in

IN THE WORD

Romans 3

Hebrews 11

2 Corinthians 5

Romans 3 as well as what it means to be a new creation in Christ in 2 Corinthians 5.

ALONE WITH GOD

What does living a righteous life mean to you?

What are some instances in your life where you have contemplated what is the "right thing to do" when it was hard to find a definitive answer? Does asking, "what is the wise thing to do" change how you would have acted in that situation?

Is the way you live your life a demonstration of right-living because of your faith in Jesus Christ?

Who is your favorite example of faith in the Hebrews 11 passage and why?

● ● ● ● **TOGETHER BEFORE GOD** ● ● ● ●

Do you feel that when we are together, we live righteously before God and act wisely in accordance with his Word?

How would you define living a righteous life?

Do you feel that together, we hold each other more accountable in our Christian walks and in our pursuit to be righteous?

Father, thank you for sending your son, Jesus, to take on the punishment for my sins so that I can live in righteousness in my walk with you.

Today, Lord, I pray that I will learn to walk in righteousness by adhering to the principles in your Word, being obedient to you and seeking your wisdom in every area of my life.

Spend some time reading through the book of Proverbs on your own throughout the course of this week. When you come across a verse dealing with wisdom or righteousness, take time to highlight it or write it on a note card.

Romans 6:13

"Do not offer any part of yourself to sin as an instrument of wickedness, but rather offer yourselves to God as those who have been brought from death to life; and offer every part of yourself to him as an instrument of righteousness."

Whatever is Pure

t's alright to be squirmy when it comes to the topic of purity. Purity is a topic that is heavily promoted but rarely talked about in detail, simply because it is uncomfortable. Let's throw it out there, the first thing that comes to your mind when I say purity is sex. Most likely that is because the church is pretty set on the idea that sex outside of the confines of marriage is wrong and sinful.

No sex before marriage, that's pretty black and white. Why? Well, because it says so in the Bible (Hebrews 13:4, 1 Corinthians 6:16). So what about hugging? Holding hands? Cuddling? Massages? Kissing? Making out? Laying down together? Feeling up? Taking the clothes off? Sleeping in the same bed (and not doing anything)? Oral sex? Or just going all the way? That is by no means a complete list, but you get the idea. You see, this idea of "no sex outside of marriage" gives your mind the ability to wander and try to figure out how far you can push the limit. At some point fairly early on in your relationship, you probably had the discussion to answer the question, *How far is too far?* This is a legitimate question and one that needs to be addressed.

God's Word is extremely clear on the idea of purity. There are constant reminders throughout the book of Proverbs that warn us against impurity and the dangers of our sexual desires. There is no question that God absolutely despises impurity. Purity is a big deal to God and it is something that you and your companion should talk very carefully and very specifically about early in your dating relationship.

There are two parts to purity and it is very important to grasp both. The first is physical purity and the second type of purity, the one referred to in Philippians 4:8, is purity of the mind. Being pure is not merely avoiding certain physical pleasures, it also means staying far away from rehearsing those scenes in your mind and avoiding fantasizing and lusting. Your thoughts are merely actions in waiting. In this study we will be taking a look at both types of temptations and how to remain pure.

Let's say I had a fresh, steaming cup of hot coffee. It was the best thing you had ever smelled in your life. The aroma wafted towards you, teasing your nose. At this point, some of you reading may be thoroughly disgusted because you hate coffee while the rest of you may be salivating because you are obsessed with coffee and were wishing that you were drinking some right now. Everybody reacts differently in different situations. The same is true in your relationship. There are going to be different things that you will do physically with your partner that will cause a different reaction. Something may arouse one of you far more than it will arouse the other individual and that is okay, because everyone is different. However, it is important to know where those temptations are and how to avoid playing near the line of what is right and what is wrong.

Guys and girls react differently. Sticking to the coffee analogy, guys are more like instant coffee. Putting it bluntly, it does not take much for a guy to get turned on. Unfortunately, the "off-switch" doesn't work as quickly as the "on-switch." Meaning, guys typically don't have great brakes and it can be far more difficult for them to stop desiring more once they have started down a trail. Girls however, they are more like coffee from a French Press. The beans have to be ground and the water has to be boiled then poured in and then the grounds and water have to seep for several minutes before it can be served as coffee, meaning girls have many components that go into being aroused and the process is often slower than that of a guy. Though these concepts are generalized and not the same in every case, they are ideas based on our emotional and psychological make-up. It is the way God has wired males and females differently. This is an extremely important concept to keep in mind because it should play a huge role on where you are going to establish physical, pure boundaries in your dating relationship.

Physical boundaries for a dating relationship are not clearly set in stone in the Bible because different couples will have different struggles. Holding hands may sexually arouse one person in the relationship while the other just views it as an affectionate gesture. It is important that together as a couple, you very specifically address situations and scenarios that will arise. It is vital that you are each very open about what will tempt you and could potentially cause you to stumble when in a physical relationship. Some people may only be able to hug until they are married because anything more could get their minds and bodies craving so much more. Others may set the boundary at holding hands or maybe at kissing. The boundaries will differ, and that is okay as long as your boundaries stay within God's standards of purity.

Our hearts and minds are dangerous. We can conjure up scenarios in our heads that lead our minds down a spiral of lust and sinful, impure desires. If you ever hear a motivational speaker talk, they will always use words like, "Imagine" or "Picture yourself." They do not just say these phrases because they sound good, they say these phrases because they work. If you imagine yourself doing something, you are far more likely to actually go out and do it.

The mind can break down even our most stubborn walls and shatter through our most concrete boundaries. Once you have your physical boundaries set, make sure that you set your mental boundaries in the same place. Do not rehearse scenarios in your mind of you going a little past the boundaries established by you and your partner. It is far too easy to undress someone very quickly in your mind or end up doing something with someone in your thoughts that you would not do in real life. The more you think on impure things, the higher your chances are to engage in lustful behaviors and actions that ultimately can bring both you and your partner past your boundaries, leaving a trail of regrets in the wake of your impurities. The mind is powerful, and the Bible clearly warns of its powers. If you are going to stumble on the road of purity, it will be when your mind has been fixated on things that are impure.

King David in the Old Testament is a prime example of someone who let his eyes wander and imagined himself with a gorgeous woman, Bathsheba. Because he was King, he could have what he wanted and he could have it immediately. So, the lustful King took another man's wife all because David had seen this lustful, steamy, intimate scenario played out in his mind.

As you spend time in the Word this week, reflect on the purity of both your thoughts and actions. Purity is tough and at times can be an awkward conversation to have with your partner. If you have already been impure in your thoughts or actions in your relationship or in a past relationship, it is not too late

IN THE WORD

2 Samuel 11-12

Psalm 51

Ephesians 5

Proverbs 20

to set a goal of purity from this point forward. God's grace is so abundant. He is quick to forgive because he is overflowing with mercy. If you've made it this far in the book, you are more than halfway done with this devotional, but that does not mean you should neglect the significance of the issue of purity. I urge you to pray and meditate on God's Word this week as you explore God's boundaries for purity as Christ-follower in a dating relationship. Learn from the failures of King David and hide God's Word in your heart when it comes to the issue of purity and temptations to be impure.

● ● ● ● ● ALONE WITH GOD ● ● ● ● ●

Do you feel that your relationship is currently pure?

If your parents ever walked in on you and your partner doing anything, would you ever be ashamed, or merely just embarrassed? There's a huge difference.

What are some safeguards you can put in place in your own life to avoid stumbling into the treacherous sin of impurity?

After reading these passages, find at least 3 other passages on purity in the Bible.

How does your perspective of purity align with God's standards for living purely?

Is there even a hint of sexual immorality in my current relationship (Ephesians 5:1-7)?

● ● ● ● **TOGETHER BEFORE GOD** ● ● ● ●

Do you feel that our relationship is pure before God?

Is there anything that I have said, done, worn or tried that has tempted you or made you stumble in your own purity?

How can I show respect to you, your parents, your emotions, your body and most importantly to God?

Is there anything we currently do physically that you believe is impure according to God's standards?

Is there anything that drops even the slightest hint of sexual impurity between you and me in accordance with God's standards?

● ● ● ● ● **PRAYER POINTS** ● ● ● ● ●

Creator of the universe and all living things, I thank you for creating the human body full of pleasures for our enjoyment. I pray that I will honor your Word and my body in my relationship and not prematurely take advantage of the gifts you have given me.

Father, guard my mind and guard my heart. Put a filter over what comes into my mind so that my heart does not desire ungodly and impure things.

Lord, when I want to be filled with physical pleasures and lustful thoughts and desires try to take over my mind, please help me to look for you because you are truly all that I need and you will give me strength to overcome these temptations.

APPLICATION

If you have not already sat down as a couple and carefully drawn very specific physical boundaries for your relationship, take the time to have that conversation. Be open and vulnerable about what will tempt you and what could make you stumble.

Create a pledge of purity that you can sign as a couple committing to be pure and accountable to one another in your relationship, but more important pure and accountable to God.

MEMORIZATION

Ephesians 5:3

"But among you there must not be even a hint of sexual immorality, or of any kind of impurity, or of greed, because these are improper for God's holy people."

Matthew 5:8

"Blessed are the pure in heart, for they will see God."

Whatever is Lovely

You may or may not be at a point in your relationship where you have said those three words, fairly insignificant individually, but together are possibly the most powerful words you can say, "I love you." Those three words are extremely profound when used together but are often tossed around lightly in today's society. Think about the word love by itself for a minute. You can love the hamburger you just ate at the local burger joint, you can go home and love your pet dog and you can go to the movie and profess your love for a celebrity on a screen that you've probably never even seen in real life, let alone actually had a conversation with.

Culture has twisted love into steamy sex scenes in movies or scantly dressed women and oiled-down, shirtless men on the cover of magazines or staring down at us from billboards. Is that love? What about all of the guys and gals that make a livelihood soliciting sex— something that God designed to be intimate, romantic and filled with passionately, binding emotion between a married man and woman—for money. That certainly cannot be love.

If you are using this study, you more than likely have professed Jesus Christ as your Lord and Savior and you desire to follow God in your relationship, so the following story is not new to you. However, instead of reading these words as a common story you have heard countless times, think about this story through a lens of love—as a love story.

Years and years ago, long before our parents or even our great, great, great grandparents were born lived a young girl, innocent and a mere teenager. God the Father, up in heaven sent an angel to this precious young child and lovingly told her that he had chosen her, out of the thousands of young woman alive, to carry and give birth to his one and only son, Emmanuel. Nine months later, after nearly losing the man she was in love with and was engaged to, Mary gave birth to a son, and named him Jesus.

Mary watched her son grow up, before her eyes. He fell down and scraped his knees, gashed open his hands, got sick and was stung by mosquitoes just like you and I did as we were children. Though he felt the same pain you and I felt, he never exclaimed out of anger or swore out of shock. He was perfect. But God had a plan for his perfect son Jesus, as he has a plan for each one of our lives. Jesus's days on this earth were numbered. You see, the only way that God could bridge the gap between mankind and himself was to send a perfect sacrifice to earth, without any sin and without shame.

So in pain, God the Father looked down on his one and only son, Jesus Christ as he was whipped and beaten to the point where even his own mother could barely recognize him through the blood and sheer disfigurement caused by the shards of metal and bones being thrust in his skin, embedded and yanked out repeatedly. The grueling process literally skinned the man alive leaving just enough lifeblood in the victim to suffer excruciating pain, but just enough not to die. God watched as his son--his perfect, blameless, righteous, truthful, noble, son--was nailed to a wooden, splintery cross, the blunt, squared nails piercing the skin through his hands and feet. The cross was then hoisted up and pushed into position in a hole, dropping several feet, so that the jolt from the cross falling into place would tear the skin even further relying on the nail stuck between the bones in the hand and the rope tied around the arms to keep the victim in place.

Mostly naked, drowning in pain and suffocating to death, our Lord and Savior, perfect and blameless, hung as a spectacle and source of entertainment for the people of that day. After suffering unbearable pain and having his own father turn away from him, Jesus breathed his last on the cross. Our sin debt was paid in full.

God watched as his son that had never done anything wrong bore the sins for the entire world. Out of love, God sent his only son to give mankind direct access to an eternity with him. That sacrifice is an act of love so far beyond what any one of us can ever comprehend.

It astounds me that we can use this word love to describe someone's outfit and turn right around and use it to describe the priceless, selfless, ultimate sacrifice that God gave to us in his son, Jesus Christ so we could have eternal life. When you think of the story of what God did for us through Jesus, it makes that word love a lot more powerful.

Think about how much you care for your boyfriend or girlfriend right now. Think about the many times you have told them how incredible they are and how much you like them. It is in those moments of euphoria when you are totally infatuated with your partner that you are able to catch just the tiniest, most minuscule glimpse of how God feels for us, as his children, each and every moment of every single day. When you see your significant other from a distance and that childish, yet beaming smile fills your face and your eyes glow and sparkle with affection and your heart excitedly starts doing somersaults inside your chest... that flood of overwhelming emotion only accounts for just a mere fraction of the way God feels for you and loves you, unconditionally, all of the time. Your love for people here on earth does not come close to comparing with the love that God has for each and every single one of those he has adopted into his family.

IN THE WORD

Romans 12:9-21

1 Corinthians 13

John 15:9-17

As you go through this week's study, the Scripture focuses on the true definition of love. Love is not some convoluted concept of sex and shallow relationships that Hollywood portrays or a verb we throw around to simulate our feelings towards inanimate, emotionless objects. Love is such an incredibly powerful word with a meaning so deep we can barely scratch its surface or understand its full meaning. Truly examine the power of love this week throughout your time alone with God and really reflect on the incredible act of love that we have been given through Jesus Christ's death, burial, and resurrection.

How does my concept of love align with the explanation of love in the Bible? How does it differ?

How has the world's portrayal of love through media affected the way I love my partner in this relationship?

I define love as...

Do I confuse the world's view of love with the Scripture's definition of love?

If I truly believe that love is patient, am I willing to patiently wait until marriage to remain pure with the partner I treasure and love?

Do you feel that I show that I like you?

Do you feel that I exemplify the biblical standards of love in the way that I treat you?

What can I do to make you feel loved and cared for?

Have we put enough emphasis on the power and the true meaning of the word love or do we use it too lightly?

● ● ● ● ● **PRAYER POINTS** ● ● ● ● ●

Father, thank you for sending your one and only son as a loving sacrifice for my sins. Help me to live in a manner that allows me to pour out your love on others just as you have done for me.

Lord, help me to understand what it means to truly demonstrate your love in my current relationship as well as with everyone that I rub shoulders with on a daily basis.

APPLICATION

Try to refrain from using the word love this week unless you truly mean the word in the context of love that is set out in the Bible.

Find a creative way to illustrate the definition of love found in 1 Corinthians 13.

MEMORIZATION

1 John 4:9-11

"This is how God showed his love among us: He sent his one and only Son into the world that we might live through him. This is love: not that we loved God, but that he loved us and sent his Son as an atoning sacrifice for our sins. Dear friends, since God so loved us, we also ought to love one another."

Whatever is Admirable

As a child, I remember putting softballs under my sleeves to make me look muscular or putting on a bath towel and calling myself Superman or singing into a toy microphone pretending to be a rock star while jamming out with my air guitar. When you were younger, you too probably dressed up like your favorite characters from a movie or book. Maybe some of you tried on your parents clothes and tried to emulate them.

The reason children dress up and try to become these characters is because kids admire something about the personas they are trying to replicate. As children, we viewed these figures as something or someone we wanted to become when we were older. This idea of admiration is something that we do on a daily basis. Sometimes we admire God's beautiful creation from the morning sunrise to the great and mighty power of an ominous thunderstorm. We may admire those who are older than we are, those who have gone before us and those who have paved the way for us. We may admire a teacher or family member or pastor. And of course we admire the person we are dating.

As we try and think on what is admirable in our Christian dating relationships, we need to have an anchor for what is actually worth our admiration. The best example of a true role model is Jesus Christ and his ministry here on earth. Though it may sound cliché, Jesus is the one and only true example of perfection that we as Christ-followers should aspire to be like. That is not to say we should abstain from admiring people here on earth for who they are, what they stand for or for the things which they have accomplished. However, the only person we should truly emulate and strive to be like on a daily basis is Jesus Christ.

The idea of admiring someone is pretty easy to grasp seeing as we idolized figures from a young age. The tougher concept to grasp is figuring out how to live a life that is admirable so that, when other people look at you they think, "Wow, that person really understands what it means to follow God" and as a result of seeing you, they desire to be more like Christ. In Matthew 5:13-16, we are called to be salt and light of the earth. These verses are calling you, as a Christian, to live your life out daily so that others will know that you are different and as a result of your representation of Christ, outsiders will want to praise and glorify and honor your heavenly father, God.

It can be difficult to understand fully what it means to live a life--- as well as be in a relationship--- that is truly worth admiring. An admirable, Christ-centered lifestyle is a compilation of what you have been studying the past several weeks. It fully encompasses right-living, having character, remaining pure, truly showing love and being true. There are so many temptations crowding you from every direction in today's society that it can be difficult to fix your eyes on Jesus as your finish line.

Several years ago, I had the opportunity to travel through the jungles of Togo, West Africa. I got to a point in the jungle where there was no trail. With only a machete we had to forge our own way through the thick foliage of the African jungle. Without a compass and without a guide, there was only one piece of advice my two fellow adventurers and I were given that would allow us to stay on the correct course and prevent us from getting lost in the jungles of Africa. The advice was simply to always stay directly between the two mountain peaks. As long as we stayed in the valley, using the pinnacle of the mountains as a guide, we would be able to safely navigate the jungle. Living lives as salt and light as well as living in this world but not as a part of this world (Romans 12:2) can be so strenuous with the pressures you face because of the sinful society of today's world. As Christians, we need those mountain peaks in our lives to help guide us in living lives that are admirable, not so we can be praised, but so people can admire God through the way we conduct our lives.

Outside of God's Word, the best earthly "mountain peaks" that we have are other Christ-followers. There are three different types of people that you should surround yourselves with in your dating relationships that will help grow you and your partner like never before. The first type of person you should surround yourself with is couples that have gone before you. These are couples that are at least a few steps ahead in their relationship. This could mean a couple that has been married for quite some time or a couple that has been dating for a substantial amount of time. They have been through the jungles ahead of you and will be able to offer you words of caution and wisdom.

The second type of person you need to surround yourself with is couples that are in the same place as you are. Find other believing couples that have put pursuing a Christ-centered, pure and godly relationship as their number one priority. These people can walk along side you, experience the same road blocks, see the same sights and climb the same hills. They can hold your hand and walk through the storms right along side you and they can run and jump through the fields when the skies are clear because they are in the same spot on their journey.

Finally, surround yourself with people that are a step or two behind you in their relationship journey. This could be couples that have just started dating or maybe even singles that are pursuing a relationship. The best way to solidify your own beliefs is to share your experiences with others. This can be accomplished as you pass along your insights and observations to people who are a few steps behind you in their adventure. As you share the highs and lows of your journey, those stories transform from your experiences to concrete pieces of wisdom and insight.

Putting those people in place in your life will allow you to be able to have your "mountain peaks" that you can look to as assurance that you are on the right trail. As you surround yourself with godly people and commit to being true and honest and asking questions and sharing insights, you will start to notice that it is easier to live a life that is admirable because you and your companion are not on the journey alone. Instead, you are walking in the company of those who have gone before, those who will walk by your side and those who are following in your footsteps just as God designed true discipleship and accountability to work.

When the world looks in on your relationship, you want to be radiating what Christ has done in and through your lives. You and your partner should desire to live in such a way that no bad thing can truthfully be said about you two. If you choose to use Christ as the center point of your journey while surrounding yourself with other, like-minded Christ-followers, your relationship will inevitably begin to honor God in the midst of this dark world. Together, you and your companion will be a beacon of light that can be admired because of what God has done for you both as a couple and you as an individual.

This week as you read, you will focus on what it means to live a life that is godly and admirable in the world in which we live. You will also see songs of praise and adoration used to worship God, our Father and our Creator, Provider and Protector.

IN THE WORD

1 Peter 2

Psalm 8

1 Chronicles 29:10-20

Romans 12:1-8

What areas of your life are currently admirable? What areas do you need to work on?

Who are some people that have gone before you and could offer insight? Who are some people that you can surround yourself with who are on the same journey? Who are some people a few steps behind you that you can share your experiences with?

What do you admire most about your partner?

What do you admire most about God?

Do you feel that you currently show your praise and adoration for God by presenting yourself as a living sacrifice?

● ● ● ● TOGETHER BEFORE GOD ● ● ● ●

Who do you admire and why?

Do you feel that our relationship would be considered admirable to onlookers?

When people look at our relationship, do we shine like a light for Christ and ultimately point people closer to God by our lifestyles and choices?

Do you think that we have conformed to the patterns of this world as a couple or have we stayed true to God's Word?

Father, help my light shine for you so that people here on earth will see my desire and passion to serve you and ultimately glorify you as a result. Please keep me humble.

Creator of the universe, faithful friend, righteous, sovereign, and merciful King, I praise you for saving me and for loving me unconditionally. Help me to be a living sacrifice, pure and holy for you.

Lord, when the pressures of this world surround me, help me to focus on you as my guide and my fortress. Let me not succumb to the luring temptations of this world but instead, please give me strength to be victorious over them so that my deeds and reputation will ultimately point others towards you.

APPLICATION

Find one story of Jesus in one of the four Gospels that you find very admirable and share it with your partner this week. Explain to them why you particularly like that attribute of Jesus.

Come up with a list of 3 or 4 attributes of God this week that you find admirable. Meditate on these attributes and integrate them into your prayer life.

Psalm 9:1-2

" *I will give thanks to you, Lord, with all my heart;*
I will tell of all your wonderful deeds.

"I will be glad and rejoice in you;
I will sing the praises of your name, O Most High."

Whatever is Excellent & Worthy of Praise

ver the past seven weeks, you and your companion have taken a look and six qualities that should all be evident and be lived out when trying to pursue a Christ-centered dating relationship. Those six character traits should begin to shape your thought processes on what it means to live out a godly dating relationship.

Each one of these traits brings you and your partner closer to being in a relationship that is excellent and worthy of praise in accordance with God's standards. Your relationship shouldn't be praiseworthy because of things you have done or because people say things like "you are a cute couple," your relationship should be praiseworthy and a celebration of the excellent works God has done in and through you as two Christ-followers who truly care about having a firmly grounded and deeply rooted understanding of what God's Word says about dating. As a couple you should make one another stronger in your faith and together you should have a greater impact for Christ's Kingdom than you would apart.

To continue to dwell on what is excellent and praiseworthy beyond this study, it is important that you meditate on the one thing that is always worthy of praise, God's Word. The verse in Philippians 4:8 is all about thoughts and training your mind to focus on what is excellent and praiseworthy.

As you continue to grow closer to God, your life should exhibit qualities that reflect the goodness of what Christ has done in your life. As a Christ-follower, your life should be overflowing with good deeds and fruit as you mature in your faith. Along the journey, there will always be battles as you face spiritual warfare. To be fully equipped for these moments when your flesh desires to be weak, it is so important to hide God's Word in your heart and memorize Scripture so that your pathway will be illuminated with the Truth and you will be able to stand firm in your faith.

This week, to conclude this eight-week study, you will be challenged to visit familiar passages throughout the Bible that deal with your faith. You will take a look at the Fruit of the Spirit as well as the Armor of God and what it means to truly hide God's Word in your heart to help you prevail through the darkest, most difficult trials and temptations.

IN THE WORD

Galatians 5

Ephesians 6:10-20

James 2:14-26

What does it mean to me to live a life that is excellent and praiseworthy?

Are my thoughts filled with God's Word so that my life will overflow with the fruit of the spirit?

Have I properly equipped myself with Scripture to stand up against the attacks of the devil?

Does the way I live my life show evidence that I am a fully devoted follower of Christ?

Do I spend adequate time alone with God allowing me to think on the excellent and praiseworthy things that He has done in my life?

Over the past eight weeks, do you feel that going through this study has helped our relationship focus on things that are excellent and praiseworthy?

After completing this study, what are some things that we can do as a couple to make sure that we keep our eyes fixed on Christ as the center of our relationship?

Out of the seven "Whatevers" what is one area that you think we should revisit as a couple that could still use a little bit of work?

● ● ● ● ● **PRAYER POINTS** ● ● ● ● ●

Lord, I thank you for your Word and the truths it holds for my life. I pray that I will apply what I've learned beyond this study to become a better companion in my relationship and more importantly, a stronger, more committed Christ-follower as a result of what I've learned. Help me to hunger and thirst to be more like you every single day.

It amazes me to think about how much you love me despite the fact you know every single good and bad thing that I have ever done and ever will do. Father, I pray today that I will focus on what is excellent and praiseworthy and strive to glorify you in all of my thoughts and actions.

Thank you so much for the incredible partner you have allowed me to be in a dating relationship with. Help me to treat him/her with respect and love and grace and mercy. Lord, I pray that I will resemble you in the way I interact with my significant other as well as with everyone I rub shoulders with every day.

● ● ● ● ● **APPLICATION** ● ● ● ● ●

If you have not already picked up another devotional to go through with your partner, it may be a good idea to start looking for one. Another option would be to go through the entire book of Proverbs. Since there are 31 chapters and 31 days in most months, you could read a chapter a day and try to outline it and pick out key verses to share with one another.

Try spending an extended time in prayer with your boyfriend or girlfriend this week. Praise the Lord for what he has done and pray for wisdom as you grow further in your relationship with God and with one another.

● ● ● ● ● **MEMORIZATION** ● ● ● ● ●

Psalm 19:14

"May the words of my mouth and this meditation of my heart be pleasing in your sight, Lord, my Rock and my Redeemer."

Psalm 119:105

"Your word is a lamp for my feet, a light on my path."

1 Corinthians 10:13

"No temptation has overtaken you but such as is common to man; and God is faithful, who will not allow you to be tempted beyond what you are able, but with the temptation will provide the way of escape also, so that you will be able to endure it."

about the book

Understanding the difficulties of pursuing a pure, Christ-centered dating relationship, I set out on a quest to find a devotional that was geared to strengthen and equip young Christian couples desiring to follow God in their dating relationship. After searching countless sources I came to the conclusion that none of the Bible studies I had looked at were exactly what I had in mind.

Using Philippians 4:8, one of my favorite verses, as a guide, I began to write this 8-week study that highlights some of the difficulties that young couples face while dating in today's society. With God's Word as the center of this devotional, I began to construct studies that would challenge the individual to deepen their walk with their Lord and Savior as well as provide a platform for couples to address serious, but relevant questions, issues and potential stumbling points in relation to their faith.

My hope is that this study will be used to encourage and equip followers of Christ to honor and glorify him in every facet of their dating relationship!

Ry

@ryancvet
www.ryanvet.com